We Can't Al

A poetry chapbook about ADHD and neurodiverge...

By Sana Burton

© 2018 Sana Burton. All rights reserved.

This book is a work of creative nonfiction, that is to say that while these poems are drawn from my own life experience, they do not involve direct recreations of events, and references to e.g. "my friend" are amalgamations and paraphrases of various people and conversations. This is because I'm pretty sure that making money off of the actual words of living humans who I did not ask permission to make money off of is probably some kind of illegal.

For Maddi, for being an enabler. For Lucinda and Louie, for putting up with me as a teenager, because teenagers kind of suck. And for Evie, for being wonderful.

Preface

I'm not a poet, or at least I don't make a habit of it. Most of what I write is prose. I kind of slipped and fell into this book. I've read a bit of poetry before, written some too, so the term "outsider art" isn't really applicable, but I don't doubt that this doesn't read like "real" poetry by "professional" writers. I say fuck too much for that, for one thing. The lack of stylistic polish is intentional; I intensely dislike the attitude of poetry being "high art" or whatever and would much rather write for broke-ass gay punk kids than for literary critics. Which, frankly, is probably apparent from the fact I named the book after a meme.

I wrote these poems about having ADHD because I feel that neurodivergent people are supposed to turn invisible after the age of 18, because I guess somebody took the "educational" part of "special educational needs" too literally. It ought to go without saying that I'm speaking only for myself, not every neurodivergent adult on the planet, but, well, Youtube comment sections exist so I guess reading comprehension is kind of on a downswing at the moment.

Ooh, shiny

If I never hear the word

Squirrel

Again in my Life

It will be too fucking soon.

Temporal Displacement

There will never be enough time

I don't know how to be
Without a deadline:

There are so many places to go
Books to read
Words to say
And I panic, because I cannot do them all.

I know, logically, that I have years
Decades
But my dopamine-deprived brain
Can't

Nothing is nowhere and everything is now
Or else will never be

Lazy

I am 10 years old and my teacher shakes her head
"You're so bright", she says
"Won't you try a little harder?"

I am 14 and can't find my shoes
"We're going to be late", shouts my sister up the stairs
It won't be the first time

I am 17 and haven't opened a textbook in weeks
I'll never get into uni at this rate
But then, what did anyone expect?

I am 23 and I take pills
That stop me from sleeping
But make me remember to do my laundry

My friend is too sad to get out of bed
Different cause, same responses
Do any of us ever actually choose to be lazy?

Language Barrier

My friend Rebecca doesn't talk

And I don't know how to sign

Her mouth and my hands

Both as useless as eachother

But we love eachother still

In text fragments

In laughter

In touch

We sit side by side

Voiceless

Our eyes telling stories

From a book none can read

Mummybloggers

I'm sick of disability narratives;

They're so goddamn melodramatic.

"My mind is a prison"?

Ha! Fuck that.

It's more like a slightly disobedient Labrador.

And if your kid can't do their homework,

Look you in the eyes,

Move out at 18,

What does it matter?

As long as you love them.

And you do love them, right?

We aren't worth less,

For having to work less.

Stop trying to make me hate myself.

Changeling

You are running, dancing, barefoot on grass
Twirling and laughing in the rain
Left their small mundane world behind
To be free as the creatures in your storybooks
For at least a while

They will try to tame you
Little one, wild one, wise one
Break your wings to fit the clothes they made you
You must not let them

Hold on to your defiance, child:
Hide cold iron with soft silk
Cultivate the fire in your eyes
Stand unapologetic when they demand a reason
A justification for your existence

Your stubborn pride will be your salvation

Isn't that, like, speed?

Stop blaming Ritalin for school shootings

You absolute fucking twats

Brain Fog

I try to listen to the words but they keep slipping

Sand through my clumsy fingers

Everything feels so distant

So faint

Where am I and why?

I close my hand over the thorns

Anchor

Check the notes scribbled on my palm

Grocery shopping. Okay. That makes sense.

I don't think the pills are strong enough

Make a mental note to bring that up

But that idea goes away too

Swept away by the fog

Like pebbles in the tide

Manic Pixie

I always relate to the characters I'm not meant to

To the fey, whimsical girls

With flowers in their blue hair

Watches on their slender ankles

Who must of course exist only for men

"How quirky", people say

Always quirky

Femme neurodivergence, distilled for your viewing pleasure

Even when they hurt it must be pretty

Bruise like poetry, cry like a kiss

Not by choice

So this is a letter of redemption

For Cassie, Ramona, and River

Who never got to be the heroes in their own stories

And for you and me, who will.

Twice Exceptional

Rewrite the same word 10 times

Count the cracks on the pavement

Triple-check the train times

Because I won't be late again, oh no

Afraid of not being perfect

Take tests just for fun, just to know

Pose, correct, overcomplicate

I'm learning three different languages

My bookshelves alphabetized and labelled

Chronic overachiever

Who am I trying to prove wrong?

Or should that have been whom?

Begin again

Begin Again

Begin Again

Special Needs

It is difficult to explain the feeling

Of growing up knowing you're broken

Hating every teaching assistant

Who only wanted to help you

But you never asked

Lying to your friends

That the physio was an after school club

And being patronized by the teachers

Who didn't read your file

Your grades

Your achievements

Let alone get to know you

Because they thought "learning difficulty"

Said enough

Gross

Its something rarely acknowledged

When you say

You have memory problems

Or bad coordination

People think of missed appointments

Late bills

Not being able to drive

They do not think of brushing hair

Cleaning teeth

Or the deep, crushing

Childlike

Sense of shame

Dyspraxia

I tripped on the stairs out of my building

The blood on my skinned hands like cherry syrup

My body doesn't work right

Exhausted from walking to the shop

Knees freeze in place when it's cold

Ankles twist at a moment's notice

I drop my bag at the station

Falling from hands

That don't remember how to grab

I count the bruises in the bath

Trying to remember how they got there

Visualising flowers in the purple

My body doesn't work right

But that's okay.

Overactive Imagination

I had invisible worlds as a kid

Hundreds of 'em

With a million secret lives contained

Enough so

That my parents thought

I was psychotic

Now that I'm older

My worlds only live on paper

As stories

I miss it being real

I want to talk to Queen Medli

I want to tell her I'm okay.

My circadian rhythms are a little bit totally fucked

I sleep for 12 hours

Or else not at all

My brain is always tired

Too much light, too much noise

To many demands to keep track of

So I feed it drugs

To make it stay alert

Always

The athlete's steroids of executive function

And if I can't let it rest when it wants to

How is it supposed to know when it needs to?

Solidarity

Too many of my friends are depressed

And I wish I knew how to help

More than I do

Sympathy not empathy

It takes one to know one

And the only experiences I can speak to are my own

And I'm sorry

But I can be angry at the world

'Cause it's a dick

On your behalf

When you're too tired to fight.

Experimental Medication

I'm thinking of microdosing acid

I say, half joking

Drugs cost money I don't have

But if I am

Defective

Neurologically speaking

Why shouldn't I have fun with it?

The pills I take

A chemical cousin to cocaine

A balancing act

My consciousness altered

From the start

Hyp(o/er)sensitivity

The light is too bright and too dull

Fuzzy

Velvet under my fingers like nothingness

Like drowning in it

Stuffy, thick

A voice just out of range

The clock ticks like rain

Death by a thousand drops

But

Sand between my toes a loving whisper

The smell of coffee a warm breeze

Sensation, displacement

Floating

The universe talks to me

In a language too strange

For these words to be enough

Queer as a noun

It is deceptively easy
To fall in love with loneliness;

To escape vulnerability
By making your heart a bomb shelter
And deflect bigots
By making yourself so weird
So in your face
That all they can do is shrug

Wear your anger as a shield
Defiant, proud, obnoxiously self-assured
Spit micro-identities like bullets
Put on your glitter as warpaint
And dare the world
To stand in your way

Existing without permission

There is a certain

Freedom

In letting yourself be inconvenient

Telling your friend

You can't watch that movie

Without subtitles

Buying fidget toys

Then losing them

And getting more a week later

Hailing a taxi

Because fuck it

Your bones hurt

Being messy and imperfect

In a society

That thinks there's only one way to be a person

Not like your child

Working in institutions is strange

When you're disabled too

You already know the right words:

Executive dysfunction

Absence seizures

Overload

You empathize in ways you shouldn't

Because you wonder where the line is drawn

I'm expected to say

I'm not that sort of disabled

I can walk

I can talk

But I won't

Because once upon a time

Being gay got you institutionalized

And IQ tests decided who can vote

Once its some of us it's all of us

You don't get to decide

Which people count as human

Hyperfocus

Have you ever loved something

So much

It becomes a part of you?

Dedication

Obsession

Purpose

Meaning

For a while at least

And

I don't understand

How something that makes me

So happy

Can be pathological

Methylphenidate diet

"You're so skinny", she says
Smile with too many teeth
"What's your secret?"

"You've lost a lot of weight, sweetheart"
Stepfather's concerned smile-frown
"I almost didn't see you there"

"I bet I could pick you up and carry you around"
Scratchy kisses from cigarette-burn lips
"It's kind of hot, actually"

I bite my lip
Not knowing what to say
"It's just the medication"

"So, like, diet pills?"
"As long as you're doing okay"
"Sweet, can I get some of those?"

I wish people would believe me
When I say I have no interest
In starving myself

Weirdo

A confession

I was the weird kid

Not the tee-hee oh-so-alternative tones of

We are the weirdoes, mister

But

The ones speculated about on Reddit

The runs-like-Naruto kid

Thinks-they're-a-faery kid

Once I forgot my underwear

On a day we had PE

I was 14

I'd come out two years earlier

Not having a reputation to lose

And I was happy

I wasn't a potential serial killer

I was just a kid

Who watched too much anime

And didn't know they had ADHD

And thought the real world was boring

Just like they thought of me

As a lost cause

Half-formed life

I sometimes feel I don't exist

'Least not outside of my head

Friends I never see

Events I never plan

Stories I never write

Too many ideas I can't make real

Manifest desire

Scrawl words on a page

Unreliable, inconsistent

Unfinished

Everything a work in progress

Always

You don't believe in me

I don't mind

Because I wouldn't either

If I was you

Cuddle piles as radical praxis

I knew I could be loved

But not understood

Make excuses, hide my truth

Neurodivergent enby turned perfect wife

But then

You call me your prince

Ring me in the morning so I'm not late

We both see other people

Live on our own

Spin apart, crash together

As our own internal orbits guide us

No value judgements

No right or wrong way to love

Just two brainfucked queers

Navigating the multiverse

Breaking all the rules

Scylla and Charybdis

For two years I couldn't live alone

Couldn't pay bills

Feed myself

Keep a house clean

I don't talk about this

For fear of losing face

No longer considered smart, capable, adult

But reduced to a tragedy

A problem to be fixed

But if I don't talk about it

Then they laugh about 'retards'

Susan's nephew with autism, ADHD, whatever

Whose poor parents just can't cope

So it's always a choice, isn't it?

Hide one side of myself or lose the other

Pick your poison

Incompetent or invisible

Low functioning or high

When we are all really both

From here to utopia*

In the future

Stores won't use florescent light

All movies will have subtitles

All books will be available in braille

We'll have ramps on every building

Sign as a universal second language

Psychotic people won't be considered scary

All medication will be free

We won't demonize addicts

Or call chronic illnesses fake

We'll stop talking about stolen children

Teach developmentally disabled folks to read

We'll all just be human

And stop trying to limit what that means

(*with apologies to Pat "the bunny" Schneeweis)

About the author

Sana Burton is a twentysomething queer currently living in Plymouth, England. They have a blog at sanaburton.wordpress.com, or else you can follow them on Twitter @sanaburton8, or look at pretty pictures they drew on sanamun.deviantart.com. This is their first book.

Manufactured by Amazon.ca
Bolton, ON